KAMP KILL KARE

MEMORIES OF LIFE IN AN ADIRONDACK GREAT CAMP

Roy E. Wires

Roy E. Wires

Outskirts Press, Inc.
Denver, Colorado

KAMP KILL KARE
Memories of Life in an Adirondack Great Camp

FOREWORD

This book is not intended to be a historical account of Kamp Kill Kare, but rather a written and pictorial accounting of the day-to-day life of a family that lived there for ten years. Books such as *ADIRONDACK CAMPS,* and *DURANT* by Craig Gilborn, *TOWNSHIP 34* by Harold K. Hochschild, and *GREAT CAMPS OF THE ADIRONDACKS* by Harvey H. Kaiser, do an excellent job of documenting the historical legacy of the Adirondack Great Camps

This book is written about the Wires family, who lived at Kamp Kill Kare from October 1964 until May 1975. My father, Edwin B. Wires served as Superintendent of Kamp Kill Kare during that period accompanied by my mother, Helen Wires. I worked at Kamp Kill Kare the summers of 1961, 1962, 1963 and 1964 prior to moving there in the fall of 1964 with my family. My sister Virginia worked there two summers and later joined us for short periods of time between education and her family commitments.

This book relates how our family dealt with living in the "back woods" at the end of a six and one half mile dirt road, and how the environment around us shaped our lives. Long before moving to Kamp Kill Kare, our family had always been an outdoors family. The opportunity to live in the deep woods came as an extension of a lifestyle we already enjoyed.

The time frame covered in this book takes place during a period when Mrs. Francis P. Garvan owned Kamp Kill Kare. Mrs. Garvan spent each summer at Kamp Kill Kare accompanied by her children, grandchildren, and other invited guests.

The experiences related in this book are real and are told as best remembered. My mother kept a journal during our tenure at Kamp Kill Kare, and this has assisted me in recounting our many memorable experiences.

CHAPTER 1

THE ROAD

As might be expected, living on the end of a six and one half mile dirt road has its highlights and pitfalls. The daily trip into Raquette Lake Village for the mail and/or supplies always had something interesting to recount. It's amazing how acute your senses become while driving daily on the same dirt road. You begin to recognize the tire tracks of others driving the same road and a strange tire tread alerts you that someone else had been there before you. Deer tracks, however common, begin to develop a pattern, indicating the presence of a regular crossing or trail. The sighting of an occasional black bear or bobcat brings you back to the reality that you live in the deep woods.

Kamp Kill Kare gate in Winter

The road and it's geography develop names such as: the first hill, the second hill, the big hill, the gravel pit, the gate house, the grassy road, the clearing, the first bridge, the second bridge, the tower, the flat; all of which assist in recounting the location of a particular experience or sighting while driving the road.

Kamp Kill Kare was responsible for maintaining the last two and one half miles of road, which began at the Sagamore barn, and continued past the fork to Uncas and through the Kamp Kill Kare gate. Sagamore maintained the road from the Sagamore barn out to the gatehouse, and the Town of Long Lake maintained the road from the gatehouse out to Route 28. These boundaries were not very definitive, and we very often helped each other out, as equipment breakdowns and weather conditions dictated.

During the deer hunting season of each year, Kamp Kill Kare, Uncas, and Sagamore, jointly employed someone to live in the gatehouse and operate a gate located on the road at the Sagamore property line. The purpose was to keep deer hunters off the properties, thereby offering some measure of protection for the large herds of relatively tame deer found on each estate.

There's always something to do on a dirt road

The seasons determined the condition of the road and the amount of maintenance required. Once the spring muddy season was over, we maintained our road with a small bulldozer, a York rake, and lots of manual labor. The damp dirt made it easy to scrape and shape the road. Large rocks that had been pushed up by the frost were either dug out or blasted with dynamite. Culverts were replaced and ditches cleaned out in preparation for summer rains. Brush and vegetation was trimmed back to improve visibility around the narrow sharp curves in the road. Once the road was graded and raked, it was ready for the influx of daily summer traffic.

Fall came and with it, a multitude of fallen leaves, which blocked the ditches and plugged culverts. It was important to make sure the ditches and culverts were clear of leaves before the snow came, as they must be clean in preparation for spring thaw. The rush of melting snow and spring rain was not the time to be cleaning ditches of packed leaves. Over the years, many ideas surfaced to make the job of cleaning leaves off the road easier. My personal contribution was the construction of a large ensilage blower on a trailer, driven by a Wisconsin gasoline engine. The discharge of the blower was directed toward the sides and ditches of the road in an attempt to blow (rather than rake) the leaves off the road. My contraption worked pretty well as long as the leaves were damp. If the leaves were too dry, a large dust cloud and billowing leaves was the result. If the leaves were too wet, the blower wasn't strong enough to move them. In any case, nature usually prevailed and it took a combination of the blower and manual labor to achieve the desired results.

Not much room

Plowing the first snow on a dirt road is usually a very noisy experience. A snowplow blade has adjustable shoes or skids on it to keep the snow plow blade itself from riding directly on the road surface. In the case of the road at Kamp Kill Kare, adjusting the shoes on the snowplow blade was necessary to allow it to ride over the many rocks that protruded above the surface of the dirt road. Unfortunately not all of the rocks escaped unscathed. More than one bone-jarring ride resulted from contact with the larger rocks. Raising the blade on the snowplow also allowed some snow to remain on the road, which in turn was then packed by vehicles traveling the road. Successive snowplowing trips allowed the road to build up, and a light thaw or rain then froze the snow packed road into a smooth surface. Once the road surface consisted of hard packed snow, it was necessary to plow the road at what some people might consider an excessive speed, however the speed was necessary to throw the snow off the snowplow blade and into the woods to keep from creating a high snow bank. If this was not done now, later in the winter, when larger snowfalls occurred, the snow banks would be too high for the plow to push the snow over, and the road would get successively narrower.

Driving the road in winter, with it's steep hills, many of which have a sharp curve at the bottom, required sharp driving skills. Freezing rain and ice kept us from our daily mail run to Raquette Lake Village on more than one occasion.

Spring thaw probably created more havoc with the road than any other season. The month of April always came with thawing and then freezing weather. It was not unusual to have a thaw, which created ruts in the road, then freeze. Following the freeze, we then drove in the frozen ruts until the next thaw, thus the expression "pick your rut, you'll be in it for the next mile!! " Spring thaw was also accompanied by rain, and is the worst enemy of a dirt road. Small washouts are to be expected, but on May 19, 1969 we had a rainstorm that dropped five and one half inches of rain overnight. This raised the lake level and washed out major sections of the road into Kamp Kill Kare. Sagamore Stream, the outlet of the lake at Sagamore, rose to flood stage, and the bridge near the gatehouse was washed away completely. All maintenance personnel from Sagamore, Uncas, and Kamp Kill Kare were on hand to keep logs and debris from jamming up against the bridge supports, but when they saw one particular large log coming, they knew that would be the end and got off the bridge. That log took the bridge with it and we were marooned and unable to cross the stream for four days.

In the end, living on the end of a long dirt road that you traverse daily, leaves much time for thought and the appreciation of the deep woods around us. It's really not all that bad.

High water took out this bridge,
but Jim Bird had it back in operation in four days

CHAPTER 2

THE SEASONS

L ife in the Adirondacks is dictated by the seasons. While most people would think of Spring, Summer, Fall, and Winter as the seasons, the year round residents of Kamp Kill Kare would be quick to include "the muddy season", and "the black fly season" as component parts of the seasonal calendar.

The author cutting ice out around the docks

The ice in Lake Kora could be expected to leave anytime during the last week of April, with spring right around the corner. Docks left in the water were cut out using a chain saw, so that ice movement in the lake wouldn't damage them. The aforementioned "muddy season" accompanies the spring thaw. One of the liabilities of living on the end of a six and one half mile dirt road is the lack of mobility when the frost leaves the ground. The dirt road into Kamp Kill Kare however manicured it might seem at other times of the year, becomes a bottomless mud pit when the road thaws, and it becomes virtually impassable for about two weeks. Certain stretches of the road become worse than others, and an assortment of vehicles is left along the road to provide a hopscotch method of transportation along those areas that have dried out. Walking the muddy areas was the only alternative. Riley Parsons in his 1929 Model A Ford however, was always one of the first to be able to negotiate the road following the muddy season.

Springtime brings with it the spring rains. A close monitoring of ditches, streams, and lake levels becomes necessary. In the spring of 1969 we had five and one half inches of rain in one overnight period. Due to runoff from the mountains, the lake level rose almost a foot and we began to worry about the high water's effect and pressure on the dam in Third Lake. During a particularly hard downpour and increasingly higher lake levels, my dad and Riley Parsons decided it was necessary to open the floodgate in Third Lake. The gate remained open for almost a week, while lake levels returned to normal.

May and June can best be described as "black fly season." While others in the Adirondacks begin to enjoy the onset of warmer weather, Kamp Kill Kare residents are enduring the black fly population. Spraying is a viable option in the more populated areas of the Adirondacks, but due to its remoteness, Kamp Kill Kare must learn to endure the pests. Those not familiar with black flies soon learn that a tar-like bug repellant, long underwear, and pants tucked into socks provide only minimal protection against these biting insects. Black flies in hoards so thick that you can hear them are the norm, and the only relief comes from knowing the season will end in late June.

Summer at Kamp Kill Kare brings with it the excitement of opening camp to the Garvan family. The road has finally dried and is graded, lawns are manicured, and deer graze on the lush vegetation. The buzz of people and the smell of wood smoke bring us to the reality that there is once again life in the deep woods.

Evening temperatures in the 40's can be expected in early September, with the knowledge that fall is close by. The Garvan family will leave shortly after Labor Day, and closing the camp becomes the task for the next few weeks. There are shutters to be put on windows, pipes to be drained, firewood to be cut and split, and building contents to be prepared for the winter. As the leaves change color and ultimately fall, raking leaves becomes an almost continuous task. The beauty of the surrounding mountains makes this one of the most enjoyable times of year at Kamp Kill Kare.

First snowfall of the year

The month of October brings with it the awareness that winter is just around the corner. The first skim of ice on the lake accompanied by a light snowfall is in order before the end of the month. By December, there is no doubt that winter is upon us and an accumulation of two feet of snow would not be out of the ordinary. Four wheel drive trucks and snowmobiles begin providing the necessary transportation. By January and February, storms have deposited three to four feet of snow and temperatures at night drop as low as forty degrees below zero. Only the cracking and groaning of the ice in the lake break the stillness of a winter's night. The northern lights dance across the sky and we gaze in awe at their beauty. Following each major snowfall, roofs must be shoveled. The greenhouses are unique in that even under two feet of snow, the heat generated in the greenhouse is warm enough to cause the snow to slide off the glass. Making sure that there is a place for it to slide to become the only maintenance task. Total snow-fall by March has no doubt exceeded forty feet, but there is comfort in knowing that April will bring with it an end to the winter.

Joel Lamphear helping out with the snow shoveling chores

The greenhouses covered up after a particularly bad storm

The Town of Long Lake gives us a hand with a bad snow drift

CHAPTER 3

THE LAKE

O n early maps and prior to development of the area in the early 1900's, the lake at Kamp Kill Kare was named Lake Sumner, but while under the ownership of Timothy Woodruff, then Lieutenant Governor of New York State, the name of the lake was changed to Lake Kora, in honor of his wife.

Lake Kora looking east towards Kamp Kill Kare

Lake Kora comprises approximately 700 acres, or physically about one mile long by a half mile wide. It is unique compared to other lakes of that size in the Adirondacks in that it is quite shallow, the main lake depth averaging only eight to ten feet. There are two islands on the lake and one of them houses a two- story log cabin, the other an open-faced lean-to.

The dam in Third Lake

In an attempt to deepen the lake, in the early 1900's a dam was built approximately one half mile down the outlet stream. This succeeded in raising the lake level about two feet and created two other small lakes known as Second Lake and Third Lake. These lakes are connected to the main lake by a small navigable channel and are somewhat deeper than the main lake, with Third Lake having a maximum depth of 24 feet.

The narrows in Second Lake looking back toward Green Top Mountain

The outlet of nearby Home Pond feeds Lake Kora, and Wakely Brook enters at Third Lake. The outlet, named Sumner Stream, flows south onto the Moose River Plains. During high water a small amount of water is diverted through a culvert, which flows through a beaver meadow to Lake Mohegan at Uncas. Lake Kora is at the approximate center of the Adirondack watershed. Sumner Stream enters a watershed, which eventually flows south into the Hudson River, and the culvert at the west end of Lake Kora enters a watershed, which flows north to the St. Lawrence River.

With the lake being so shallow in depth, the resultant warm water temperature will not support a native trout population, however it does support a thriving population of smallmouth bass. It is my understanding that the purpose of the dam on the lake outlet and the resultant increase in water depth was done in an attempt to establish a trout and landlocked salmon population. There is no evidence that either species survived. A mounted landlocked salmon, caught by Mr. Garvan and hanging on the mantel in the Boathouse Office serves as the only reminder of an attempt to introduce this species into the lake.

Being an avid scuba diver while living at Kamp Kill Kare, I spent many hours scouring the lake bottom. The log cribs which once supported a bridge to the cabin on the island are still in existence about three feet under the water's surface. I spent quite a bit of time diving in Third Lake as it was the deepest. The dam also houses a large floodgate with the inlet being approximately ten feet under the surface. I annually inspected this four feet square concrete tunnel for logs or other debris, which might become lodged in the gate if it were ever opened.

As an enthusiastic fisherman I always wanted to believe that there was a small brook trout population in Lake Kora. I had caught brook trout in

Home Pond outlet, which also served as one of the inlets to the lake, as well as Wakely Brook, which flowed into Third Lake. Brook trout were plentiful in Sumner Stream outlet and I even caught and transplanted a few over the dam however a few trout probably does not constitute a population. No doubt there is an old rogue brook trout in the lake somewhere, but neither my scuba diving nor my angling efforts ever disclosed his whereabouts.

A Lake Kora smallmouth bass

CHAPTER 4

Employees

The staff at Kamp Kill Kare can essentially be divided into three categories: full time employees, summer employees, and domestic help for the Garvan family.

Some of the Summer of '63 maintenance men

Full time employees consisted of my father, Edwin B. Wires who was the camp superintendent, my mother Helen Wires, who assisted with all aspects of camp operation including cooking for the younger children in attendance during the summer; an electrician and maintenance man who during this era was Riley Parsons accompanied by his wife Phyllis. I also spent a number of years working full time as a maintenance mechanic.

Tony Harper from Raquette Lake did carpentry work

Summer employees were usually hired to begin working around the first of May. This summer crew of 4-6 men, usually consisted of retired carpenters, lumberjacks, and general handymen. Some of the "regulars" who returned for many seasons were Walt Bellinger, Irv Kelpy, Joe Perrier, Seward Beach, Tony Harper, and Art Jenkins. Most came from the Forestport area, with one or two from the Raquette Lake area. A cook and housekeeper for the Men's Camp also began work at the same time. Clara England served as the cook for the Men's Camp for many years, assisted by Evelyn Longway, and later Laura Petrie. In addition, three college age boys were usually hired to begin work in June. Their jobs consisted of general maintenance work until Mrs. Garvan arrived, at which time two of the boys served as bellhops, and one as a boat boy/lifeguard. The college age boys worked through the Labor Day weekend, with the balance of the men and Men's Camp staff staying on until firewood was cut in October. A night watchman was also employed during the time Mrs. Garvan was in attendance to keep a watchful eye on fireplace fires.

The domestic help was generally hired by Mrs. Garvan and most came from the New York City area. They consisted of a butler, a parlor maid, a kitchen girl, a "first cook" for the family and guests, a "second cook" for the domestic help, a chambermaid, and two chauffeurs. William "Willie" Renzetti, was Mrs. Garvan's personal chauffer and Johnny Jankowski was the second chauffer. Both had been with Mrs. Garvan for many years.

Kamp Kill Kare still had a number of old crank-type telephones with bells, which had been converted for internal communications. Each of Mrs. Garvan's employees had a particular ring, such as one long and one short ring for the chauffer, two long rings for a bellboy, etc. You just cranked the phone the required number of rings, and then picked up the earpiece and spoke into the mouthpiece mounted on the wall. It was antiquated, but it was effective and in keeping with the décor.

Periodically, additional persons were hired to assist with special projects such as the annual wood cutting and splitting operation.

CHAPTER 5

Animals

As one might expect, living in the Adirondack Wilderness brings with it an abundance of animals of all types. From the ponderous black bear to the tiny deer mouse, each has its own place in the wilderness.

As a family, we didn't consider ourselves novices when it came to familiarity and identification of the animals that surrounded us. Our many summer vacations to Raquette Lake, combined with the forestry occupational background of my father, and our family's general love of the outdoors made us quite knowledgeable of animals and animal lore.

You never knew where you might find a fawn

One of the more obvious animals at Kamp Kill Kare is the white tailed deer. The local population however, fluctuated with the season. During the summer, there were approximately ten deer that stayed around the camp most of the time. They felt comfortable enough around us that they gave birth to fawns on the front lawn and were always at the back door begging for a handout. During the winter months, the deer population exploded to thirty to forty deer. Many were there to escape the deep snow in the woods, but most were there to get their supplemental feeding of "Trim." Trim is a horse feed product, which we purchased from the Agway store in Boonville. The danger in feeding deer in the winter is that it brings many deer into a concentrated area, so we were especially careful to put out sufficient quantities of food to enable all deer to get their fair share. It wasn't unusual to wake up in the morning and see deer covered with the night's snowfall, laying in the back yard, waiting for their daily ration.

Feeding Time!!!

My dad would go out and bang on the bottom of a bucket with the feed scoop, and the surrounding woods would come alive with deer prancing in, their heads and tails held high. There were a number of deer that spent the night across the lake in the Hardwood Notch, and it wasn't unusual to see half a dozen deer come running across the frozen lake at the sound of the scoop banging on the bucket. One winter we had a fawn that we named Poor Pitiful Pearl, who was very emaciated and we knew that she would not survive the winter. The other deer in the yard were also very aggressive towards her and would not allow her to get to any of the piles of feed. In an effort to save her, my dad built a small shelter out of hay bales for her on our porch. She wound up sleeping there every night, and my dad would feed her individually. In the end, she survived the winter and within a couple of years, turned out to be the largest doe in the herd.

To the inexperienced eye, all deer look the same, but such is not the case. Most all of the regulars had names like Fanny, Gorgeous, Mrs. Murphy, Mrs. Harwood, Scamp, and the list goes on. Each one had facial features that distinguished them from the others. For example, Mrs. Harwood had short rounded ears, as did her offspring. We called her Mrs. Harwood because she came from the west end of the lake down the Harwood Trail. Most of the "regulars" we saw for four to six years before they apparently died of old age. Each would bring their new fawns to the back door, as if to introduce them to us. It was not unusual to see three generations of deer, all with the same mother, feeding in the backyard at the same time.

Fanny with one of her fawns

Got anything for me?

Papa the 8 point buck

Doe or female deer were the predominate deer around camp. The fall rut attracted bucks in pursuit of the does, but they generally stayed out of camp, however one particular old gray-faced buck we named Papa made appearances every fall for about three years. During the rut, you had to be especially careful, as buck deer can be aggressive and very unpredictable. An eight pointer attacked Bruce Darling, the caretaker at Sagamore, one year and chased him into the house. We saw many fawns that turned out to be bucks, but most did not stay around after their first year. An exception to this was Thumper. Thumper was one of Fanny's offspring, and I guess she told him that we were okay, because he adopted us and developed into almost a household pet. If Thumper was around, and you opened the kitchen door, Thumper, the four point buck, would just walk right in, and casually stroll into the living room and nuzzle my dad for a handout. Thumper was about three years old the last time we saw him.

Thumper, the household pet, with Helen Wires

Black bears, while not plentiful, were common enough to be seen almost daily at the camp dump during the summertime. Most of the time, the bears stayed in the woods, but occasionally they would come into camp. One of the more common occurrences was at the Men's Camp. Mrs. Clara England, the Men's Camp cook, spent most of her waking hours cooking and preparing the day's meals. I guess the smell of her good cooking was more than the bears could stand, and they would hang around outside her kitchen. Once in a great while, one of them would try to pull the screen door off, but Mrs. England would throw a pail of water on them through the screen, and they'd go running off. In severe cases, we'd call Frank Lamphear, the local Game Protector, who would bring one of his live bear traps in, and catch a bear or two and relocate them to another area in the Adirondacks. This usually took care of problem bears. One particular runt of a bear we named "George". George was probably two years old, but didn't weigh more than one hundred pounds. He'd hang around our cottage, cleaning up after the deer had had their morning pancakes. (Yes, my mother always had to make an extra pancake or two for the deer). Eventually George got "too friendly" and was relocated to another area of the Adirondacks, coincidently Lake George.

George, the Black Bear

Every Adirondack camp has its raccoons, and Kamp Kill Kare was no exception. The greatest concentration of raccoons seemed to be in the area of the barn. Many holes existed where log construction met the huge rocks from which the barn was constructed. The raccoons would squeeze through these holes, which allowed them access into the void between the interior and exterior walls. Decades of raccoon generations were reared in these areas. You could walk quietly up the stairs to the second story over the garage and horse stables, and hear the baby raccoons in the walls squealing over each other. A knock on the wall quickly ended the squealing and brought forth a growl from mama raccoon. As might be expected, when full grown, the raccoons roamed all over the camp. We had our regular night visits to the kitchen windowsill, which usually contained a few suet scraps for the birds. On more than one occasion we were startled by a "masked bandit" peering in our window. One particular night we were awakened by a clanging and banging coming from the small wooden box built around our garbage can. It seems that a raccoon had managed to lift the hinged lid up and get inside, but the lid fell back down, trapping him inside. When dad went out to investigate, all he could see was this little hand sticking out from under the lid, searching for some sort of latch. That was one happy raccoon when dad opened the lid.

For quite a few years each October, we had a small flock of Canada geese land on the lawn near the playhouse and feed on the lush green grass. They usually stayed for three or four days before continuing south. It was comforting at night to hear them out on the lake quietly talking back and forth to one another. One particular year, on a beautiful warm fall day, they all took off honking their goodbyes, and we awoke the next morning to find the ground completely covered with snow. I guess their instincts could tell bad weather was coming.

Loons were also regular summer lake inhabitants, and a small brood was usually raised over in Second Lake each year. Their mournful cry is as much a part of the Adirondacks as the mountains themselves.

Porcupines have very few natural enemies, and roamed freely throughout the area. We did upon occasion; have to exercise a measure of control, as they had a tendency to be attracted to and chew on the log buildings. I remember one particular night when we were awakened by a loud scraping noise on our cottage. Closer investigation the next morning showed that a resident porcupine had stopped by for a few gnaws on a corner log.

Beaver frequented the lake, but were inclined to stay away from populated areas, so most confined their activities to Second and Third Lakes. At one time beaver did present a problem and were climbing on the lawn and chewing on a group of white birch trees. In an effort to control these late night excursions, each tree was circled with wire mesh to keep them from leveling the landscape while we slept.

Bobcats are very shy animals, but tracks in the snow proved them to be frequent visitors to the camp. We were always concerned that a bobcat would kill one of our deer, but never found any evidence that one had.

Fisher were almost extinct in the Adirondack Mountains at one time, however, their population has made an excellent comeback. We often saw tracks in the area, however a fisher roams hundreds of acres while on the prowl, and it may be weeks before they return. The fisher is one of the few natural enemies of the porcupine. They know how to lie in wait for an old "quill pig," and at just the right moment, flip them over, attacking the porcupine's underside, which has no quills.

Coyotes started making a comeback in the Adirondacks in the early 1960's. From a boat, I once observed a mother and two pups following the shoreline in Second Lake. Every once in a while the mother would point her nose into the air and howl and the pups followed suit. It was almost like she was teaching them how to howl. Once in a while, we heard them howling at night, and were fearful that they might attack our deer herd, but that was never to be. When the deer were feeding in the back yard, we occasionally would see them all stare into the woods, start stamping their feet nervously, their ears rotating like a radar antenna, and we were suspicious that a coyote might be nearby. George Brownell, the caretaker at Uncas shot a coyote one fall, and dad saw two of them crossing midway down the lake on the ice one winter, but we never saw any near camp.

Mink inhabited the area, as evidenced by tracks and sign, but these elusive animals avoid human contact as much as possible. I did however see a pair of them chasing each other on the front lawn one time. They were acting just like kids, running, jumping, and squealing.

Otter were quite scarce in our area. They are known for traveling long distances and occasionally in the winter, I would see tracks where they would run and slide in the area around Wakely Brook or Sumner Stream, but I never saw any animals.

In addition to the often seen Red Squirrel and Snowshoe Rabbit, the Deer Mouse was always evident. These little creatures seem to find their way into every nook and cranny available. We were always opening up a box or a drawer and finding a deer mouse nest in the corner. The unfortunate part is the nest was usually made from what ever was present in the drawer or box. More than one towel was found shredded for nest material.

George Brownell with an Adirondack coyote

The wild animals of the Adirondacks serve as our seasonal calendar. The deer's coat changes color from the ruddy red of summer, to the gray of winter and also thickens to provide them protection against the harsh Adirondack winter. The snowshoe rabbit's fur changes from a summer brown to white in winter, offering it camouflage against predators. The weasel changes its color and its name from being brown in summer to being called an Ermine in winter with it's white fur. When living deep in the woods, it's not necessary to keep track of a paper calendar anyway. Let the animals tell us what month it is.

CHAPTER 6

TRAILS IN THE DEEP WOODS

L iving on the fringes of the Adirondack wilderness brought with it a deep desire within me to explore the surrounding forest. When I first arrived at Kamp Kill Kare in 1961 I used to gaze in awe at an old U.S. Geological Survey map located on the wall of the Men's Camp. It was a brownish colored map dating from the 1930's or 40's and located on it were all the old trails, which originated in the early 1900's. Of course the great blow down of 1950 obliterated most of these trails, but the adventurer in me made me wonder if any of these old trails could still be found. I talked with Riley Parsons about the existence of some of these old trails, and he shared with me his knowledge along with a few stories, which only furthered my desire to do some exploring.

Home Pond from up on Green Top Mountain

One of my first explorations was the trail to Lost Brook. The trailhead originates in the little clearing just past the church, and continues about two miles to the brook. Actually Lost Brook is the inlet to Sagamore Lake, and the trail intersects the stream in its upper headwaters. The trail to the stream appeared to be traveled frequently by black bears, as many of the trees along the trail had been chewed as the bears marked their territory. An interesting note here, when black bears follow a trail, they also tend to follow in the footsteps of the bears that preceded them. Consequently, it is not unusual to find deep paw print depressions in a trail that is used frequently by bears. The trail to Lost Brook is one of these although I never saw a bear on the trail. The trail begins in a balsam and hemlock forest, giving way shortly to a maple and beech hardwood forest. The remnants of an old sugar bush shack from days gone by greet you as you approach the stream. I never did find out what era the sugar bush originated in. The brook trout in Lost Brook are always eager to take a fly or small spinner, and a frying pan full is almost guaranteed. A small spring bubbles out of the ground where the trail meets the stream, providing a cool drink for the return trip. The Lost Brook trail was usually trimmed about once a year, as the Garvan family and guests frequently went fishing there.

Another trail that has been maintained over the years is the trail to Home Pond. This trail of about a mile in length, originates at the end of the woodshed and follows the trail around the lake for a short distance before branching off to the left. It travels through a dense balsam and hemlock forest most of the way before opening up at the perimeter of the pond. A small rustic bench sits on the top of a small knoll overlooking the pond. The outlet of Home Pond meanders through a beaver meadow at the foot of Green Top Mountain before eventually flowing into Lake Kora.

The USGS map at the Men's Camp showed a trail that continued another two or more miles past Home Pond, to a small pond called Aluminum Pond. Many stories flourished about the fantastic brook trout fishing in Aluminum Pond, so that was one of the places I sought to locate an old trail. The map showed the trail leaving Home Pond and going up the north slope of Wakely Mountain, leaving the balsam lowlands for the hardwood forest. I did find the remnants of an old trail crossing the beaver dam on the outlet of Home Pond. I was able to follow it only for a short distance before the undergrowth absorbed it. . A couple of old glass telephone line insulators and some copper telephone line told me I was probably on the right track, as an old 1940's telephone line to the fire tower lookout on Wakely Mountain was supposed to follow a portion of the trail to Aluminum Pond. I'm afraid the trail to Aluminum Pond has long since reverted back to Mother Nature and the deep woods.

Ed Wires at Stillwater Camp

Much of my interest in locating old deep woods trails comes from my desire to fish some of these long forgotten spots. One that seemed to have great promise was the old trail to the Sumner Stream Stillwater. This trailhead is located just to the left of the culvert at the west end of Lake Kora. This particular trail carried with it many stories about its use over the decades. One individual referred to it as the old "military trail." He suggested that this trail was one that was used by Sir William Johnson who fled through the Adirondacks to Canada during the American Revolution. One usage a bit more current refers to it as the "Harwood Trail," in reference to Len Harwood of Inlet, who used this trail going to his wilderness camp on the Moose River Plains to the south

In any case, this trail did appear to be a bit wider than most others I had explored, easily big enough for a wagon and team of horses. The trail maintained its width all the way down to a large white birch tree, which coincidently is also the Kamp Kill Kare property line. From that point on, it became a footpath only. It is interesting to note, that although this trail had not been maintained for many years, and the balsam and hemlock undergrowth had closed in on the sides, the animals of the forest still used it often enough to keep a slight depression and path visible on the forest floor. The existence of old corduroy logs across a few wet places, also gives some creditability to the fact that at one time wagons were probably used on this trail. About two miles down the trail, there is a fork, and a smaller trail turns to the left. This trail leads to the head of the Stillwater. It was very near this fork in the trail that I found an old blue and white porcelain cup where a spring rivulet crosses the trail and I hung it on a nearby branch. I also found an old canoe rack with an old broken canoe on it, sitting on the edge of the woods where the trail to the left meets the head of the Stillwater. The canoe probably originated from a period back in the early 1900's when the Garvan family did quite a bit of fishing and outdoor camping. The Stillwater itself is a natural pooling of water, and is about one half mile long, sixty feet wide, and the water is two to three feet deep. Large brook trout were plentiful, and quite a bit of beaver activity was observed. The edges of the Stillwater are quite swampy and make for very difficult walking. Back in the woods, if one were to continue straight ahead on the main trail, it emerges at the south end of the Stillwater where once again the water picks up speed and flows over a rocky streambed on it's way to the Moose River. There is also evidence of an old bridge at this location, no doubt to assist the wagons in crossing the stream. On the east bank of the Stillwater, I found an old broken-down boathouse, which probably housed the boats and canoes used by Stillwater visitors. Old maps of this area also showed a small camp on the Stillwater, and on one of my fishing trips to this area, I knew I couldn't go back until I found it, or at least where it had been. After considerable slogging up the east bank and past the old boathouse, I came across a small stream flowing out of a balsam thicket. A short distance up the stream I found a narrow footpath, which led me to the still standing, legendary "Stillwater Camp." The camp consisted of a very small log cabin approximately 10 by 12 feet, and an open faced log lean-to with a tin roof. The door had long since been torn off its hinges, probably by a bear, and the porcupines had eaten holes in the floor, but the roof was still intact. The open-faced lean-to still had bedrolls and pots and pans suspended by wire from the roof beams. It was quite obvious that many generations of mice and squirrels had lived in the bedrolls over the years. On a later trip to Stillwater Camp, I spent the night there. While gazing into the evening campfire, I couldn't help but think back to the time when the Adirondack wilderness was first opened, and what person might have been sitting on the same rock as I was, in total and complete defiance of city life, while enjoying the bountiful beauty of the Adirondack Wilderness.

Sumner Stream Stillwater in Winter

There is also another old trail that leads to the Stillwater. This trail originates just over the dam in Third Lake, and is visible for a short distance on the east side of the Sumner Stream outlet. There is evidence of an old fish hatchery at the beginning of the trail, however the trail is soon lost in a big beaver meadow about a quarter mile below the dam. Travel to the Stillwater is easiest in the winter on snowshoes by just following the outlet stream south.

During my Dad's tenure as Superintendent at Kamp Kill Kare, we refrained from doing any maintenance of the trail to the Sumner Stream and Stillwater Camp. The State of New York had recently opened the Moose River Plains Wilderness Area to the general public for hunting and recreation use, and it was our fear that a manicured trail in that area would lead a hunter north to Kamp Kill Kare and potentially threaten our deer herd.

Although it never appeared on any map, at one time there was a trail that went to the summit of Green Top, the mountain overlooking Kamp Kill Kare. I was never able to find anything resembling a trail, so I decided to cut one of my own. The trail I cut begins behind the Men's Camp and continues uphill through a reforested area, giving way to a hardwood ridge. The trail then enters an evergreen forest and proceeds steeply up the southwest slope ultimately reaching the summit. I cleared an extensive area on the top, which when looking south, permits a full view of Kamp Kill Kare, Lake Kora, Home Pond, and the surrounding wilderness.

An interesting short hike is a trail to a slightly elevated area known as the Hardwood Notch. It branches off from the lake perimeter trail directly across from the Boathouse. This is an area that over the years has survived the logger's saw. It contains a stand of large yellow and white birch and a few very large hemlock trees. The deer seem to enjoy this particular sheltered area in the wintertime with its plentiful browse.

I think my fondness for exploring the trails of the deep woods lies in knowing that decades ago, these trails were used by those that enjoy the solitude of the deep woods as much as I. The forest wildlife and those that come after me will serve to perpetuate these paths.

The Adirondack wilderness from up on Greentop Mountain

CHAPTER 7

LEISURE TIME ACTIVITIES

It's hard to imagine living in the deep woods without having hobbies or enjoying activities associated with your surroundings. Having been raised in a family that enjoyed the outdoors only developed my interests further, the difference being, the outdoors was now my backyard.

We may often use the term outdoorsman too loosely. To me, an outdoorsman is a person that not only enjoys being in the woods, but one that can appreciate the smell of the balsams, the gurgling of a stream, and the sight of a far off mountain. It's a person that goes fishing and catches nothing, but still considers the day a success because they saw a pair of beavers working on their lodge. It's the person that goes hunting, and enjoys watching an industrious chipmunk storing food for the winter, or hears the pat, pat, pat of a partridge drumming in the distance. It's the person that is constantly aware of their surroundings and misses nothing and absorbs everything.

My outdoor activities have always included fishing, and my residency at Kamp Kill Kare was no exception. For all practical purposes, the small mouth bass in Lake Kora had never seen a lure, and eagerly attacked most all presentations. I certainly caught my share of bass in the lake. Other fishing expeditions included trips to Lost Brook and down Sumner Stream for brook trout. Occasionally, my dad and I would get into Lake Sagamore for some early season brook trout, or to Lake Mohegan in Uncas for Lake Trout. My dad did catch a nice ten-pound lake trout on one trip to Lake Mohegan. I also fished Sagamore Stream for brook trout, and was especially fond of "The Uncas Hole", which was where the outlet of Lake Mohegan met Sagamore Stream.

Fall brought with it, the rustle and crunch of fallen leaves, and my thoughts turned to the harvest of a buck deer and venison for Mrs. Garvan. Being sensitive to the fact that we had a deer herd of our own made me hunt in areas far away from Kamp Kill Kare. Most years either my dad or I were successful in bagging a buck deer for shipment to Mrs. Garvan's butcher. After the deer was harvested and dressed, it was shipped intact to New York City by railroad. I understand Mrs. Garvan never ate venison herself, but gave it away to her friends. My dad once had occasion to talk with the butcher, and he said he had the biggest collection of deer antlers in New York City in his shop.

The author with a Lake Kora smallmouth bass

The coming of fall and winter also brought with it a desire to roam the woods and set out a trap line. With the trap line also came with it the obligation to check the traps on a daily basis, and snowshoes or snowmobiles became the mode of transportation. The surrounding state land provided an untapped wilderness for trapping, and this is where we concentrated our efforts. A winter trap line usually rewarded us with bobcats, fisher, and beaver. Between attending the trap line, and preparing the pelts, it certainly helped to pass the long winter days and nights.

Ed Wires with a nice 10 pound Lake Trout from Uncas

The advent of the snowmobile certainly permitted our family to enjoy the outdoors more during the winter season. Of course, there were also occasions after a major snowstorm when a snowmobile was the only method of transportation, but we enjoyed riding them for recreational use as well. Areas of forest that were impenetrable on foot during the summer now became accessible by snowmobile during the winter. A degree of caution had to be used however, as it was possible to get many miles from home, only to have a mechanical failure and have to leave the snowmobile and walk back home. A small backpack of rations and a pair of snowshoes became standard equipment on long excursions. A favorite trip of my dad and I was the ride into Uncas, and then on down to Bear Pond Camp. Bear Pond Camp was a piece of privately owned land belonging to a group of sportsmen in Old Forge that was originally an old logging camp, but they had since fixed it up and used it as a hunting camp.

This nice buck is headed to New York City

Another long snowmobile trip that I often made started at the Kamp Kill Kare gate, went into Uncas, and then down the old Uncas Road that comes out on Route 28 across from the entrance to Eighth Lake State Campsite, through the campsite, down the length of frozen Eighth Lake to the canoe carry to Browns Tract Ponds, from Browns Tract Ponds up the old railroad bed to Raquette Lake Village, through the village to Route 28 and Sagamore Road, and then Sagamore Road back to the Kamp Kill Kare Gate and home. That was a long, but always enjoyable trip.

Unfortunately, not all hunters are woodsmen, and some occasionally get lost. While spending the night in the woods may seem like a serious affair, law enforcement officials don't consider someone lost until after they have spent two nights in the woods. The rational is that many individuals walk into the woods too far during the day to get back out before nightfall, and wind up spending the night and walking out the next day. In those cases where someone has spent two nights in the woods, an effort is made to form organized search parties to assist in locating the missing individual. Search parties are often made up of locals who know the country, the local Conservation Officer, Forest Ranger, and the State Police. I often participated in these search parties when needed. One large search in particular occurred in October 1966 and was for a young man by the name of Peter Gade from Syracuse, New York. This teenager had been bow hunting on the west side of Sagamore Road and was lost somewhere between there and Eighth Lake. After about four nights out, this search party turned into a major search effort, with busloads of students from his high school in Syracuse, and a New York State Police bloodhound team participating. On the seventh day, after six nights in the woods, Peter Gade was found alive huddled under a blow down and was airlifted out by helicopter. A happy ending to a search that was beginning to look like it would end in unpleasant circumstances.

Another time George Brownell, the caretaker at Uncas, (which was owned at the time by the Rockland County Boy Scouts), called my dad to tell him that they had twenty scouts and two leaders that had been lost for two days and for us to be on the lookout for them. Buster Bird, a bush pilot from Inlet, finally located them from his airplane down on the Sumner Stream Stillwater, and dropped a note to them in a soda can telling them where they were and how to get out. We met them in boats at the west end of the lake and took them home. No doubt that adventure made for some great stories around the scout campfire.

The Moose River Plains was a vast area of wilderness south of Kamp Kill Kare and down the Sumner Stream outlet. Because I was knowledgeable of that section of the forest, I once accompanied Gary McChesney, the Raquette Lake Forest Ranger on a search for two lost hunters in that area. We walked from the west end of Lake Kora all the way down to the road that went from Limekiln Lake into the Moose River Plains. This search also had a pleasant ending as the hunters were found on the third day.

This big bobcat weighed 25 pounds

An Adirondack Fisher

Ed Wires with a nice beaver

Living in the deep woods away from other people, shopping centers, and entertainment, requires you to either love the woods or leave it. The early explorers of the Adirondack wilderness were true woodsman who could appreciate what God had created. Those that came after developed it so others could appreciate it as well, and those that eventually settled here were looking for a place away from the hustle of city life. They knew what they were looking for............and they found it in the Adirondacks.

Bear Pond Camp

CHAPTER 8

OPENING CAMP

With the melting of snow and ice toward the end of April, our thoughts begin to turn to the opening of the camp. As the snow melts, it reveals a mat of leaves and tree trash, which must be raked up to allow the grass to grow. Thinking, "we just did this", makes us count the months and we soon realize that it's been six months since the first snow fell. Dad has been in touch with last year's employees, and most are ready to come back for another season. Riley Parsons turns on the water and checks out the boiler in the Men's Camp in preparation for the arrival of the cook, housekeeper, and about six men around the first of May. It's been a long winter and everyone is ready to get back to work.

The lawn and paths are raked first. This gets rid of the winters mat, and helps the drying process. Dad and I have already been raking and grading the road, but this time of year it has to be done about every four or five days, as it is still very wet and must dry out. Ditches are cleaned and dug out in preparation for the seasonal rains. The frost has pushed up a few big rocks, which are dug out or blasted with dynamite, and a couple of loads of dirt may be necessary to fill an occasional low spot. Once the roads and paths are shaped up, our attention turns to the buildings.

Most windows are covered with large wooden battens to protect them from the winter's blast. These battens are heavy, and require the full crew to manhandle them off the windows and put them into storage.

Riley Parsons has turned on the water to most of the buildings. In spite of adequate preparations, seals have dried out and there are a few small leaks. Due to the change in temperature, the stone walls and electrical boxes in the Main House basement are covered in condensation, so lacking heat, Riley has to wait until things dry out a little bit before he can turn on the electrical power.

Mother starts a regimented process of airing out the buildings by opening the doors each morning. A walk after supper brings with it a time to close   the doors for the night.

Spring house cleaning takes on a whole new meaning when looking at the scope of buildings that must be prepared for the coming season. Mother usually hired a couple of women from Raquette Lake to assist with this task. Doris Lamphear and Pat DeMarsh helped for many years.

The process of setting up each building exactly the way it was the previous year became a bit more involved. The first year we were at Kamp Kill Kare, mother and dad took pictures of each room, noting where each polar bear skin rug went, where each picture sat on a desk, and how each room was arranged. Following the spring cleaning, mother would set up a slide projector as she moved from room to room, and using the slide picture, would put each room back exactly the way it was the year before.

Close inspection of the exterior of the buildings usually revealed boards or whole porches that needed replacing, logs that needed to have bark replaced, and other repairs caused by the ravage of the winters snows.

Firewood for fireplaces was stockpiled in or near each building, and each fireplace (36 of them if I recall) had firewood put in them, ready for lighting by the room's first occupant. Each fireplace also had to have its own supply of "fuzz sticks", which were pieces of clear white pine kindling, that had had long, thin curls shaved on it using a spoke shave. Walt Bellinger was an expert at this, and on rainy days could usually be found up in the carpenter shop making these unique fire-starting items.

Activities around the Boathouse and dock area usually involved painting the boats and later putting them in the water and allowing them to swell, thereby making them watertight. Buoys were also put out on some of the rocks in the lake to keep persons boating and unfamiliar with the lake out of danger.

Dad's annual flowers had now grown large enough to be transplanted from the greenhouses into window boxes and flowerbeds. The challenge now became keeping the deer from eating the flowers. Temporary fences were put up, but somehow the deer always managed to clean out a few plantings. What the deer ever saw in eating a bitter marigold, I'll never know.

The final polish before Mrs. Garvan arrived was edging and raking all the paths. This final touch always became her first visual impression as she returned to Kamp Kill Kare after a ten-month absence.

CHAPTER NINE

THE BUILDINGS

M uch has been written about the construction and buildings at Kamp Kill Kare. This chapter is intended only to relate our observations and experiences as it pertains to those buildings.

Stone archway going into barn area

One of the more interesting buildings at Kamp Kill Kare is what is fondly referred to as "the barn". This complex was constructed out of massive stones quarried on site. Close scrutiny of the northwest side of Green Top Mountain, reveals areas where stone was quarried and was no doubt used in the barn's construction. The barn complex consisted of a carpenter shop, a blacksmith shop, garage, stables, carriage spaces, a cow barn, and a lumber- room. While horses were once kept in the stables, there is no visible evidence that cows were ever kept in the cow barn, and it appears that this area was used primarily for dry storage. A silo was also included in the complex.

Men's Camp

About 200 yards uphill and across from the silo is the springhouse. This house is actually a screen house, which encloses the natural spring water supply. The spring itself is surrounded in laid up stone and the spring water is seen bubbling up through the sandy bottom of a shallow pool. The spring water then gravity flows through a three inch pipe for about a quarter of a mile to a pump house and reservoir where it is stored before being pumped up to two larger storage reservoirs at a higher elevation up on the mountain. Water pressure is derived entirely from gravity pressure. An interesting experience occurred during my first summer working at Kamp Kill Kare. While living in the Men's Camp, I had no access to refrigeration, and desiring to keep some soft drinks cool, I put them in the spring. It wasn't long before Riley Parsons, while monitoring the reservoirs, noticed that the water levels were low and went up to check on the spring. Unfortunately, one of my soft drink cans had floated up and was restricting the water flow in the pipe to the reservoir. As might be expected, I had to find another place to keep my drinks cool.

Playhouse

Colonial fireplace area in Playhouse

About one hundred yards behind the barn, there is an old stone foundation. I was told that this foundation was the remains of Kamp Keen Kut. This building was built in the early 1900's and is reportedly to have been used exclusively by men guests during that era.

The Men's Camp is a two-story, heated log sided building, where the summer employees who worked on the grounds lived. During the time that the Garvans were in residence, the chauffeurs also stayed there. This building had the potential to house 25 or 30 men, but usually housed only 6 or 8 plus a cook and housekeeper.

Immediately behind the Men's Camp was a root cellar built back into the side of the mountain. It contained two rooms and was used to store the cook's vegetables. Interior temperature was usually around fifty degrees.

Superintendents Cottage

There were two other log sided buildings that were used as residences for full time employees. One of these contained electrical monitoring panels, and was the residence of Riley Parsons.

I found the remnants of an old wood frame building up on the side of the mountain behind the Men's Camp. It appeared that it might have been an old maintenance building, as I found wooden nail kegs, maple tree taps, and fence wire in the area.

The farm was located on the north side of Green Top Mountain. All that remains is a small tool shed and some concrete frames used in growing plant seedlings.

At the foot of the hill and on the lakes edge, is a small covered dock known as the Help's Dock. This was a place where servants and other employees could go to swim and relax.

The main camp is all located near to the lake. Coming down the road from the barn, and just past the Help's Dock, the first building seen is The Playhouse. This log sided building sits behind home plate of the baseball field. It contains a two-lane bowling alley, a squash court, an old English pub, and an early colonial living area. Adjacent to the bowling alley portion of the building are two clay tennis courts. These courts were high maintenance items, but the Garvan family and their guests thoroughly enjoyed using them.

Next to The Playhouse was the Superintendents Cottage where my family and I lived year round. Connected to the log sided Superintendents Cottage with a common front porch was the log sided Children's Cottage. These cottages had central heat and were available for occupancy year round. The Children's cottage was so named because the younger Garvan grandchildren stayed there. Meals for the adult family members were often too lengthy for the children to sit still though, so my mother cooked for the children when they were in residence.

Behind The Playhouse was The Power House. This stone-faced building contained the standby generator and was the hub for all electrical service. At some point in the early 1900's, an attempt was made to provide direct current electrical service to Kamp Kill Kare through the use of lead acid storage batteries. There were still numerous large glass trays in The Power House, that once contained the acid and plates that had been used in this endeavor. The standby generator was an old four cylinder Kohler gasoline engine that often needed repair. Lyman Appleton from Old Forge, was called upon whenever major repairs to the generator were necessary. It was within minutes of the completion of a valve job on the Kohler engine one time, that the lights went out and the generator started up automatically. While we were still in amazement at the timing of such an event, we soon learned that the entire Northeast United States was without electrical power that November 9th, and was soon to become known as the "The Great Northeast Blackout Of 1965."

A short distance behind The Superintendents Cottage was a stone-faced building called The Pump House. All sewage and wastewater from the entire facility flowed by gravity to a large underground concrete vault, which was easily as big as the room in a house. A very old and large three-piston pump with cannonball sized check valves, was then used to pump the vault's contents through a six-inch iron pipe up and over the rock face of Green Top Mountain and into a drain field above the farm. This whole process was a major construction and engineering feat, considering it was designed and built during the 1930's, and in spite of minus 40 degree temperatures in the wintertime, the line never froze. The six hundred foot change in elevation from the pump house to the drain field was sufficient to create sixty pounds of back pressure on the pump check balls when the system was shut down. It was not a pleasant sight when the pump check ball housing broke one time, and the entire contents of the pipe ran back down into the pump house!!

The Church is a magnificent structure, built from solid stone quarried out of Green Top Mountain. Inside are white plaster walls with hand forged iron gates built on site. My mother did the flower arrangements, which were changed frequently. Father Jude, the resident priest serving Inlet and Raquette Lake, conducted Sunday Mass in the church for many years, and was a frequent guest of Mrs. Garvan.

Church

Church Altar

Four glass Greenhouses provided roses and other cut flowers for the church as well as for building window boxes, flowerbeds, and flower arrangements in the buildings. My father raised all flowering annuals from seed, this task beginning in late April while there was still snow on the ground and ice in the lake. We never had what you would call a gardener on staff, those duties all being performed by my father. The roses at Kamp Kill Kare received widespread notoriety, as prior to the arrival of the Garvan family for the summer, roses by the dozens were given to local friends and merchants from Raquette Lake to Old Forge. My dad always said he wished he could delay the rose crop a little longer, as the biggest crop of roses came just a few weeks before the arrival of the Garvan family. Standing adjacent to the greenhouses was a beautiful two-story stone-faced gardeners house, which remained unoccupied for many years.

Greenhouses and Gardener's house

One of four greenhouses

Roses were given away by the dozens all the way to Old Forge

The Boathouse was a log sided building, which was actually three stories high, the first story being at waterfront level and used for dockage and storage of boats and motors, the remaining two stories being living quarters and a large office. The waterfront level also contained a very old carbon arc movie projection camera, booth, and cloth screen. I understand, that many years before, the showing of old family movies from the 20's and 30's was a popular pastime at night. In addition to fireplaces, this building was also heated, and provided living quarters for the Garvan family if they came during the off-season. During our tenure at Kamp Kill Kare, most of Mrs. Garvan's grandchildren were quite young and enjoyed water activities. After a long period of minimal motorboat activity due to a motorboat accident years before, and as the lifeguard and boat boy at the time, I convinced Mrs. Garvan to allow me to teach the grandchildren to water ski. I brought my own water skis and equipment from home, and in the summer of 1961, taught over 20 people how to water-ski.

The Boathouse from the lake

Boathouse from the main lawn

The Boathouse office

Adjacent to the Boathouse was the log-sided Main House, which contained living quarters for all domestic help, a laundry, the kitchen, dining room, and living quarters for guests. Many rooms in this complex had unique names such as the Indian room, the bird room, the dog room, and Patsy's room, obviously named by either who or what occupied them. Off from the main dining room was a smaller octagon shaped room, which was appropriately named the Octagon Dining Room. The Main House was built on a sloping grade; consequently you had to traverse sets of stairs as you walked from one section or room to the next. At its highest point, the Main House connected to a large room with high ceilings known as The Casino. No doubt it received its name from the many card games that were played there over the years. In its present form however, it served as a room where the Garvan family enjoyed a cocktail before dinner, played a little pool, or just sat before the large fireplace.

The Main House

The main dining room looking toward the octagon dining room

The main dining room and six foot wide fireplace

Next to the Casino was a log sided building with a screen porch known as Mrs. Garvan's cottage. This building contained upstairs living quarters for her personal maid, a downstairs office, and personal living quarters for Mrs. Garvan. The bedroom contained the infamous "tree bed", which was a tree trunk complete with owls and birds in the branches, which served as one of the bedposts.

The entrance to Mrs. Garvan's cottage

Mrs. Garvan's office with polar bear skin rugs

In front of the Main House and adjacent to the waters edge were two open-faced lean-tos. These lean-tos were filled with soft, interlaced balsam boughs and Hudson Bay blankets, and provided a place for an occasional "campout" for the children.

The island in the lake directly in front of the Main House, contained a two-story log faced building known as the Kabin. This seldom-used building contained a small library and other artifacts. At one time a bridge connected the island to the mainland, but has long since been torn down. The log cribs supporting the bridge however, are still visible under the water.

Woodshed with overhead dry storage

A large woodshed adjoins the lawn across from the greenhouses. This woodshed was usually filled to about half it's capacity of 500 cords at the beginning of each summer season. One end of the woodshed has an upstairs complete with a tin lined room. It is in this tin lined room that all the trunks containing bear skin rugs and the like are stored during the off- season. The tin lining was supposed to make it "mouse proof" although I doubt that anything can lay claim to that title!

In addition to all the aforementioned buildings, there was also a log sided icehouse, walk-in coolers, and a stone maintenance shed. There was a network of manicured sand paths and roads connecting many of these buildings, and it was the job of the grounds employees, to constantly rake these paths, keeping them free of leaves, pine needles, and footprint traffic. It was humorous to see some guests walk on the grass to keep from making a fresh footprint on a newly raked path.

The buildings at Kamp Kill Kare however ravaged by fire twice in their history, remain both solid in their construction as well as their heritage, and stand strong as an example of one of the Adirondack Great Camps.

CHAPTER 10

THE END OF AN ERA

The death of Mrs. Francis P. Garvan in 1979, brought with it, the end of an era in which those persons with the means to own and maintain a Great Camp in the Adirondacks was slowly coming to an end. Some of the other camps and estates in the Adirondacks have been donated to various non-profit organizations and educational institutions, however Kamp Kill Kare is one of the last to survive.

Unfortunately, as many pieces of real estate similar to Kamp Kill Kare become available and for sale, the State of New York buys them for a pittance, destroys the buildings, and attempts to return the land to "forever wild." This concept, while good in theory, leaves no room for perpetuating the heritage and legacy of the great camps.

I'm afraid the days when families gathered together at their summer retreat in the Adirondacks has been lost to the concrete and asphalt of city life. The wealthy and not so wealthy no longer have time, or are willing to take the time, to enjoy what God has created for us. The Adirondacks will be here forever.............we will not.

Printed in the United States
83842LV00004B/415-462/A